THIS JOURNAL BELONGS TO:

_____

the courage to be seen

A JOURNAL FOR UNDERSTANDING YOUR STORY TO REWRITE YOUR FUTURE

BY JORDAN DISANJH

All Rights Reserved

© [2025] [Jordan Disanjh]

No part of this book may be copied, reproduced, stored in a retrieval system, or transmitted in any form or by any means—electronic, mechanical, photocopying, recording, or otherwise—without the prior written permission of the author, except for brief quotations used in reviews or articles.

This book is for personal use only. Unauthorized distribution or resale is strictly prohibited. The content within is based on personal insights and is not intended as professional advice.

For permissions, inquiries, or publishing rights, please contact: thecouragetobeseenbook@gmail.com [Jordan Disanjh].

I AM MADE OF MEMORIES

—Madeline Miller

WELCOME

This journal is not the solution. It will not fix anything. I am not a psychologist, so I really do not know what I am talking about. But talking, writing, and sharing my story has allowed me to evolve by looking at some hard truths and experiences. It has allowed me to lay everything on the table in front of me, look at everything, and realize that I want to grow and that I can grow. I want to use my experiences whether good or bad and grow from them. This is why I created this journal, I think anyone can grow, so if these activities helped me then hopefully they can help you as well!

Most of these questions are things that I have asked guest after guest on my podcast, The Transparently Jordan Podcast. All my guests are always so brave and answer these questions openly and honestly. I thought if they can be so brave and speak their truth to a stranger, then we all can surely have the courage to be just as vulnerable.

When you start this journey, be prepared to get stuck! In fact, I want you to get stuck! I want your chest to tighten, I want it to become hard to swallow, I want you to laugh, cry, and I want you to dig deep. One piece of advice is, if you get stuck, try your best, then come back to the activity the next day and try again!

I hope you enjoy this journey! I hope you rise after this journey. I hope that after this journey you always hold your head up high and always have the courage to be seen.

Jordan

LIFE ISN'T MEANT TO BE LIVED ON PAUSE

Stop waiting for the perfect moment— there isn't one. Chase your dreams, take risks, and embrace every experience, because time moves whether you do or not. The only thing worse than failure is looking back and realising you never even tried.

THE POWER OF WRITING

Writing is a powerful tool for self-expression and reflection, helping you organize your thoughts and process emotions. It allows you to communicate ideas, preserve memories, and connect with others, making it an essential practice for personal and creative growth.

Day 1

Date: _____

Let's start by practicing some writing. Spend 5 minutes and write down a personal biography. Do not worry if you get stuck we will try this again later during this journey.

_____
_____
_____
_____
_____
_____
_____
_____
_____
_____
_____
_____
_____
_____
_____
_____
_____
_____
_____
_____
_____

REFLECTION & IMPROVEMENT

It is important to reflect about the past. Improvement only comes when we know what can be better and we do not know that until we reflect.

Day 2

Date: _____

What things in the past have shaped the way that you see things now or go about your life? Set a timer and reflect for 2 minutes. Then set another timer for 3 minutes and list your thoughts.

BUILD EMOTIONAL RESILIENCE

Our emotions are essential signals that provide insight into our inner world, guiding us toward understanding our needs, desires, and values. Taking time to reflect on them helps us process experiences, build emotional resilience, and cultivate a deeper connection with ourselves and others.

Day 3

Date: _____

List all the emotions that you feel the most often. Now pick 3 of the emotions from the list and write down some times, places or experiences when you felt those emotions. Are there any patterns? If the emotion you listed is positive how can you create opportunity to feel that emotion more. If the emotion you listed is negative, how can you prevent that emotion from arising?

PERSONAL QUALITIES

Reflecting on our personal qualities allows us to recognise our strengths, identify areas for growth, and align our actions with our values. This self-awareness fosters personal development, helps us build authentic relationships, and empowers us to navigate life with greater purpose and confidence.

Day 4

Date: _____

What is a personal quality of which you're most ashamed? How can you look at that personal quality a bit differently?

WORK ON DEFLECTION

Looking down on others often stems from insecurities, as it can be a way to deflect attention from one's own perceived shortcomings. It's easier to judge others than to confront internal struggles, but true confidence comes from self-acceptance, not comparison.

Day 5

Date: _____

Write down what makes you look down on other people. Why do you look down on these things?

_____
_____
_____
_____
_____
_____
_____
_____
_____
_____
_____
_____
_____
_____
_____
_____
_____
_____
_____
_____
_____
_____
_____
_____
_____
_____
_____

HANYA YANAGIHARA

"And so I try to be kind to everything I see"

Vulnerability Practice   Date: _____

Lets take a break and practice reflection in a different way! Answer the following prompts in 2-3 sentences.

What is a core memory from your past?

_____

_____

_____

Who are the main people involved?

_____

_____

_____

Where does the story take place?

_____

_____

_____

How does this memory make you feel?

_____

_____

_____

What have you learned from this memory?

_____

_____

_____

_____

STOP CARING WHAT OTHERS THINK

Not caring what others think about you is freeing, as it allows you to live authentically without seeking validation. When you prioritize your own values and happiness, you gain the confidence to make choices that align with who you truly are.

Day 6

Date: _____

What do you think makes other people look down on you? Do you think you would change these things that you think others look down on?

START LOVING YOURSELF

Loving yourself is essential because it sets the foundation for your well-being and how you interact with the world. When you embrace your worth, flaws, and strengths, you cultivate inner peace and build healthier relationships with others.

Day 7

Date: _____

What do you most like about yourself? Spend 5 minutes to write down your thoughts.

_____
_____
_____
_____
_____
_____
_____
_____
_____
_____
_____
_____
_____
_____
_____
_____
_____
_____
_____
_____
_____
_____
_____
_____

YOU BRING VALUE TO THIS WORLD

People are drawn to you because you bring something truly unique to the table—your perspective, talents, and energy are one of a kind. The world benefits from your originality, and those around you appreciate the authenticity and value you bring to every situation.

Day 8

Date: _____

What do you think makes others like you? Spend 5 minutes to write down your thoughts.

FEAR

We are hardwired to feel fear - it's what keeps us safe, after all - but most of us are also prone to inappropriate fears; fear of failure, fear of speaking in public, fear of leaving a bad relationship, whether personal or professional. Inappropriate fears have no positive purpose and the first step to overcoming them is to know what they are.

Day 9

Date: _____

Make a list of everything you're afraid of and, as you list your fears, think about how they make you feel.

STEPPING OUT OF YOUR COMFORT ZONE IS HARD BUT IT IS SO WORTH IT

Stepping out of your comfort zone is where real growth begins. It's about embracing uncertainty, facing fears, and challenging the limits you've set for yourself. While it may feel uncomfortable at first, it opens the door to new opportunities, greater resilience, and a deeper understanding of your true potential.

Day 10

Date: _____

What's a moment in your life when you felt completely out of your comfort zone, and how did you grow from it?

EMBRACE FAILURE AND DON'T QUIT

Failure may be the opposite of success but it is a crucial part of the journey toward success. Each setback teaches valuable lessons, builds resilience, and helps refine your path. Embracing failure as a learning opportunity allows you to grow stronger and be more prepared for future challenges.

Day 11

Date: _____

Share a time when you felt like you failed at something important? What did you learn from that experience?

_____
_____
_____
_____
_____
_____
_____
_____
_____
_____
_____
_____
_____
_____
_____
_____
_____
_____
_____
_____
_____
_____
_____
_____
_____
_____

FIND YOUR PEOPLE

There's something deeply comforting about being seen for who you truly are—no pretending, no filtering, just you. It feels like a warm embrace, a quiet validation that you are enough exactly as you are. When someone recognises and accepts your true self, it creates a sense of belonging that is both freeing and uplifting.

Day 12

Date: _____

Who was the first person to truly see you for who you are, and how did that change your life? Spend some time creating a storyline of what happened during this time.

LET IT GO

Letting go of old beliefs can feel unsettling at first, but it also creates space for growth, clarity, and new possibilities. When we release ideas that no longer serve us, we free ourselves from limitations and open the door to a more authentic, fulfilling life.

# Day 13

Date: _____

What's a belief you once held about yourself or the world that you've since had to let go of?

DON'T GO THROUGH IT ALONE

Asking for help not only lightens your burden but also strengthens connections, reminding you that you don't have to face everything alone.

Day 14

Date: _____

Was there a time when you had to ask for help but struggled to do so? What did that experience teach you about connection?

WHAT'S YOUR STORY?

Everyone carries a personal story shaped by their experiences, struggles, and triumphs. No two stories are the same, yet each one holds meaning, resilience, and growth.

Day 15

Date: _____

What's a part of your story that you've only recently found the courage to share? Why now?

RISE TO THE CHALLENGE

Overcoming your lowest point shows you just how strong and resilient you truly are. It may not have been easy, but every step forward proved that you were capable of growth, healing, and renewal. Looking back, you can see how that challenge shaped you into the person you are today—wiser, braver, and more compassionate.

Day 16

Date: _____

Can you write about a time when you were at your lowest and what helped you rise back up?

BE MORE KIND TO YOURSELF

Self-compassion means treating yourself with the same kindness and understanding that you would offer a friend, allowing space for growth, mistakes, and healing without self-judgment.

Day 17

Date: _____

What's a lesson you've learned about self-compassion that you wish you could share with your younger self?

WHAT IS YOUR TRUTH?

Overcoming the feeling of being misunderstood starts with embracing your own truth, even when others don't fully see it. As you grow in self-acceptance, you begin to attract people who truly understand and appreciate you. In time, you realise that being misunderstood doesn't diminish your worth—it simply means your perspective is unique and valuable.

Day 18

Date: _____

Have you ever felt misunderstood in a significant way? How did you navigate that experience?

FORGIVENESS AND LOVE

Forgiving yourself is a powerful act of self-love, allowing you to release guilt, learn from the past, and move forward with kindness and grace.

Day 19

Date: _____

What's something you've forgiven yourself for, and how did it impact your sense of peace?

BENJAMIN ALIRE SÁENZ

"Words were different when they lived inside of you."

Day 20

Date: _____

You did it! You put it all out there! Now lets go back to day 1. **Spend as long as you need and write down a personal biography.** *Once you have finished go back do day 1. See the difference? Looking back on your past allows you to recognize patterns, learn from mistakes, and celebrate progress, giving you a clearer sense of direction. Reflection helps you understand who you are, what drives you, and what adjustments you need to make to move forward with greater purpose and confidence.*

Day 20

Date: _____

Day 20

Date: _____

THANK YOU

Thank you for purchasing the journal! I hope you enjoyed this journey! Be sure to give the official instagram of The Courage To Be Seen a follow!

@thecouragetobeseen

ACKNOWLEDGEMENTS

Picture credits: ©[francescooch] via Canva.com cover page, 3; ©[yayaore] via Canva.com 15, 17, 19, 21, 23, 25, 27, 29, 31, 33, 35, 37, 39, 41, 43, 45, 47, 49, 51, 53, 55, 56, 57; ©[septh5th Studio] via Canva.com 1, 5, 10, 11, 12, 13, 14, 16, 18, 20, 22, 24, 26, 28, 30, 32, 34, 36, 38, 40, 42, 44, 46, 48, 50, 52, 54, 58, 59

p. 7, Copyright © Madeline Miller, The Song of Achillies

p. 24, Copyright © Hanya Yanagihara, A Little Life

p. 54, Copyright © Benjamin Alire Saenz, *Aristotle and Dante Discover the Secrets of the Universe*

www.ingramcontent.com/pod-product-compliance
Lightning Source LLC
Chambersburg PA
CBHW071916070526
44583CB00016B/2018